Themes For Women's Day Programs

Themes For Women's Day Programs

Ann M. Eggleton

Copyright © 2010 by Ann M. Eggleton.

Library of Congress Control Number: 2010914087
ISBN: Softcover   978-1-4535-8136-0
              Ebook   978-1-4535-8137-7

All rights reserved. No part of this book may be reproduced or transmitted in any form or by any means, electronic or mechanical, including photocopying, recording, or by any information storage and retrieval system, without permission in writing from the copyright owner.

This book was printed in the United States of America.

To order additional copies of this book, contact:
Xlibris Corporation
1-888-795-4274
www.Xlibris.com
Orders@Xlibris.com
82744

CONTENTS

9	FAMILY REPOSSESSING THEIR POSSESSIONS
10	IT'S PRAISE TIME IN THE FAMILY!
11	WOMEN OF GOD, FOLLOWING GOOD THINGS
12	WOMEN, KINGDOM BUILDERS FOR CHRIST
13	WOMEN OF GOD, USING THE POWER OF GOD
14	GODLY WOMEN, SOWING SEED
15	HOLY WOMEN, STANDING IN PRAYER
16	HOLY WOMEN, IMPLEMENTING GODLY PRINCIPLES AND HOLINESS IN THESE LAST DAYS
17	HOLY WOMEN, STRIVING FOR THE GOLD
18	HEAR THE CRY, HEED THE CALL
19	WOMEN, IMPLEMENTING GODLY PRINCIPLES AND HOLINESS
20	MISSIONARIES: BE INVOLVED
21	MISSIONARIES, STEPPING OUT AND PROCLAIMING CHRIST
22	SPIRITUAL DEVELOPMENT
23	MISSIONARIES, "WORKING TOGETHER WITH ONE MIND"
24	WOMEN OF GOD, "USING PRAYER EFFECTIVELY"
25	ACCENTUATE THE POSITIVE AND ELIMINATE THE NEGATIVE
26	HOLY WOMEN, "SOLDIERING CHRISTIAN ARMOUR"
27	WHAT KIND OF CLOTHES ARE YOU WEARING?
28	WOMEN OF GOD, IN THESE CHANGING TIMES
29	FRUIT OF THE SPIRIT
30	WHO CAN FIND A VIRTUOUS WOMAN?
31	HOLY WOMEN IN THE HALL OF FAME
32	WOMEN OF GOD, SOWING SEED
33	WOMEN OF GOD, "USING THE POWER OF GOD"
34	"GODLY WOMEN, RUNNING THE RACE IN THE 21st CENTURY"
35	WOMEN OF GOD, "VICTORIOUS IN A HOSTILE SOCIETY"

36	WOMEN OF GOD, "CONQUERORS THROUGH CHRIST"
37	THE POWER OF PRAYER, CHANGING SITUATIONS
38	WOMEN OF GOD, "STAND UP AND BE COUNTED"
39	WOMEN OF GOD, "USING PRESCRIPTIONS FOR A GODLY LIFE"
40	THE POWER OF PRAISE
41	WOMEN OF GOD, "EMPOWERED TO SERVE"
42	WOMEN IN THE WORD, CLAIMING VICTORY
43	HOLY WOMEN, BEARING FRUIT
44	WOMEN STANDING IN PRAYER
45	GODLY WOMEN, "SETTING A GOAL"
46	MISSIONARIES TOTALLY COMMITTED
47	CRY OF A GODLY WOMAN: "LORD, TEACH US"
48	THE THREE ASPECTS OF PRAYER
49	PRAYER, PRAISE AND POWER TIME
50	WILL THOU BE MADE WHOLE?
51	WOMEN OF GOD, WEATHERING THE STORMS OF LIFE
52	MOURNING WOMEN IN ACTION
53	GODLY WOMEN WITH POWER, OVERCOMING TEMPTATIONS
54	ERNESTLY CONTEND FOR THE FAITH
55	THE TOTAL WOMAN
56	THE CHRISTIAN WORKERS OUTFIT CLOTHED IN RIGHTEOUSNESS
57	HOLY WOMEN OF GOD, WALKING BY FAITH!

POEMS

60	WHAT HAVE YOU DONE FOR JESUS?
61	CONSIDER
62	ALMOST PERSUADED TO BE A MISSIONARY
63	GET SOMEBODY ELSE
64	TRAVELING ON MY KNEES

all things are possible if you
BELIEVE   Faith

Hope   Let love and faithfulness
never leave you.
~ Proverb 3:3

God Bless

Show me your ways, oh Lord,
teach me your paths, guide me
in your truth and teach me.
~ Psalms 25:4 - 5

PRAY
God's listening

Praise   BLESSING

Blesses are the pure in heart,
for they will see God.
~ Matthew 5:8

FAITH is God's work in us

That everyone may eat and drink,
and find satisfaction in all his toil.
this is the gift of God.
~ Ecclesiastes 3:13

DEDICATION: This book is dedicated to all "Women of God" who are mission workers for Christ, and especially to my best friend and 'sister,' the late Mary Lou Halton.

FAMILY REPOSSESSING THEIR POSSESSIONS

Sub-Topic: It's Time to Fight Back

Panel Discussion

1. In the Home
2. In the Schools
3. On the Job
4. In the Church

Reference Scripture: For the weapons of our warfare are not carnal, but mighty through God to the pulling down of strong holds: II Corinthians 10:4 KJV

IT'S PRAISE TIME IN THE FAMILY!

Sub-Topic: A Call to Praise!

Panel Discussion

1. Youth Leaders
2. Family Leaders
3. Church Leaders
4. Choir Leaders

Reference Scripture: Let everything that hath breath, praise the Lord. Psalm 150:6 KJV

WOMEN OF GOD, FOLLOWING GOOD THINGS

Sub-Topic: Having Faith in Action

Panel Discussion

1. Righteousness

2. Godliness

3. Patience

4. Love

5. Meekness

Reference Scripture: Let us therefore follow after the things which make for peace, and the things wherewith one may edify another. Romans 14:19 KJV

WOMEN, KINGDOM BUILDERS FOR CHRIST

Sub-Topic: How Are You Building?

Panel Discussion

1. Prayer Builder (Hannah)

2. Missionary Builder (Dorcas)

3. Faith Builder (Esther)

4. Unity Builder (Ruth)

5. Building Destroyer (Sapphira)

Reference Scripture: And are built upon the foundation of the Apostles and prophets, Jesus Christ himself being the chief corner stone. Ephesians 2:26 KJV

WOMEN OF GOD, USING THE POWER OF GOD

Sub-Topic: Authority: Do You Have It?

Panel Discussion

1. Difficult Situations
2. Spiritual Power
3. Overcome Temptation
4. Miracles of Healing

Reference Scripture: But ye shall receive power after that the Holy Ghost is come upon you. Acts 1:8 KJV

GODLY WOMEN, SOWING SEED

Sub-Topic: How Do You Sow?

Panel Discussion

1. Seeds by the Wayside

2. Seeds upon the Rock

3. Seeds among Thorns

4. Seeds on Good Ground

Reference Scripture: Sow to yourselves in righteousness, reap on mercy, break up your fallow ground. Hosea 10:12 KJV

HOLY WOMEN, STANDING IN PRAYER

Sub-Topic: Lord, Teach Us To Pray

Panel Discussion

1. Intercessory Prayer
2. Congregational Prayer
3. Individual Prayer
4. Travailing Prayer

Reference Scripture: For everyone that asketh receiveth; and he that seeketh findeth; Luke 11:10 KJV

HOLY WOMEN, IMPLEMENTING GODLY PRINCIPLES AND HOLINESS IN THESE LAST DAYS

Sub-Topic: The Witnesses of Our Faith

1. Panel Discussion

2. Christian Warfare

3. Denying Ungodliness

4. Suffering Persecutions

5. Chosen Generation

Reference Scripture: But as He which hath called you is holy, so be ye holy in all manner of conversation. I Peter 1:15 KJV

HOLY WOMEN, STRIVING FOR THE GOLD

Sub-Topic: Don't Hinder Me!

Panel Discussion

1. Loins Girt About with Truth
2. Breastplate of Righteousness
3. Shield of Faith
4. Helmet of Salvation

Reference Scripture: I press toward the mark for the prize of the high calling of God in Christ Jesus. Philippians 3:14 KJV

HEAR THE CRY, HEED THE CALL

Sub-Topic: Who Will Answer the Challenge?

Panel Discussion

1. Meeting the Needs of the People

2. Limitations

3. Expectations

4. Referral and Follow-Up

Reference Scripture: Then said I, Here am I; send me. Isaiah 6:8 KJV

WOMEN, IMPLEMENTING GODLY PRINCIPLES AND HOLINESS

Sub-Topic: Be Steadfast

Panel Discussion

1. Chosen Generation I Peter 2:9

2. Christian Warfare Ephesians 6:13-17

3. Denying Ungodliness Titus 2:11-12

4. Suffering Persecutions II Timothy 3:11-12

5. The New Creature II Corinthians 5:17

Reference Scripture: But as he which hath called you is holy, so be ye holy in all manner of conversation: I Peter 1:15 KJV

MISSIONARIES: BE INVOLVED

Sub-Topic: Mission Accomplished

Panel Discussion

1. Visit the Prospect

2. Prison/Jail Ministry

3. Telephone Ministry

4. Becoming Involved

Reference Scripture: Whatsoever thy hand findeth to do, do it with thy might. Ecclesiastes 9:10 KJV

MISSIONARIES, STEPPING OUT AND PROCLAIMING CHRIST

Sub-Topic: He's Worth Going After

Panel Discussion

1. The Challenge
2. The Value of a Soul
3. Going Where He Is
4. Effective Witnessing
5. Harvesting the Product

Reference Scripture: And when he hath found it, he layeth it on his shoulders, rejoicing. St. Luke 15:4 KJV

SPIRITUAL DEVELOPMENT

Sub-Topic: Are You Growing?

Panel Discussion

1. Lust of the Flesh
2. Lust of the Eye
3. Pride of Life
4. Maturity

Reference Scripture: And have no fellowship with the unfruitful works of darkness, but rather reprove them. Ephesians 5:11 KJV

MISSIONARIES, "WORKING TOGETHER WITH ONE MIND"

Sub-Topic: Target Power

Panel Discussion

1. Stand Fast

2. In One Spirit

3. With One Mind

4. Striving Together

5. For the Faith of the Gospel

Reference scripture: That ye stand fast in one spirit, with one mind, striving together for the faith of the gospel. Philippians 1:27 KJV

WOMEN OF GOD, "USING PRAYER EFFECTIVELY"

Sub-Topic: Teach Me Lord

Panel Discussion

1. Learning How to Pray

2. What is Prayer?

3. When I Pray

4. Empowered by Prayer

Reference Scripture: Praying always with all prayer and supplication in the Spirit. Ephesians 6:18 KJV

ACCENTUATE THE POSITIVE AND ELIMINATE THE NEGATIVE

Sub-Topic: Add to your faith and lay aside unbelief

Panel Discussion

1. Virtue and Knowledge—I Peter 1:5

2. Temperance and Patience—I Peter 1:6

3. Godliness and Brotherly Kindness—I Peter 1:7

4. Charity—I Peter 1:7

Reference scripture: But he that lacketh these things is blind, and cannot see afar off, and hath forgotten that he was purged from his old sins. II Peter 1:9 KJV

HOLY WOMEN, "SOLDIERING CHRISTIAN ARMOUR"

Sub-Topic: Survival

Panel Discussion

1. Whole Armour   Ephesians 6:13

2. Loins   Ephesians 6:14

3. Breastplate   Ephesians 6:14

4. Feet   Ephesians 6:15

5. Shield   Ephesians 6:16

6. Helmet   Ephesians 6:17

7. Sword   Ephesians 6:17

Reference scripture: And that ye put on the new man, which after God is created in righteousness and true holiness. Ephesians 6:24 KJV

WHAT KIND OF CLOTHES ARE YOU WEARING?

Sub-Topic: Durable Clothing

Panel Discussion

1. Clothing of Fasting and Prayer
2. Clothing of Silk—Strength and honor
3. Sheep's Clothing
4. God's Clothing

Reference scripture: And her merchandise and her hire shall be holiness to the Lord. Isaiah 23:18 KJV

WOMEN OF GOD, IN THESE CHANGING TIMES

Sub-Topic: It's Praying Time

Panel Discussion

1. Praying In the Home

2. Praying on the Job

3. Praying for Leaders

4. Praying in the Church

Reference scripture: If my people, which are called by my name, shall humble themselves and pray and seek my face, and turn from their wicked ways: II Chronicles 7:14KJV

FRUIT OF THE SPIRIT

Sub-Topic: Acceptable Fruits of God

Panel Discussion

1. Joy
2. Peace
3. Longsuffering
4. Gentleness
5. Goodness
6. Faith
7. Meekness
8. Temperance
9. Love

Reference Scripture: For the fruit of the Spirit is in all goodness and righteousness and truth: Galatians 5:22 & 23KJV

WHO CAN FIND A VIRTUOUS WOMAN?

Sub-Topic: For Her Price is Far Above Rubies

Panel Discussion

1. She openeth her mouth with wisdom

2. She looketh well to the ways of her household

3. Her children arise up and call her blessed

4. The heart of her husband doth safely trust in her

Reference Scripture: Who can find a virtuous woman? For her price is far above rubies. Proverbs 31:10KJV

HOLY WOMEN IN THE HALL OF FAME

Sub-Topic: Faithful Women

Panel Discussion

1. Sarah—Woman of Motherhood

2. Mary—Woman of Mission

3. Ruth—Woman of Faith

4. Hannah—Woman of Prayer

5. Dorcas—Woman of Service

Reference Scripture: Woman received their dead raised to life again, and other were tortured, not accepting deliverance, that they might obtain a better resurrection: Hebrews 11:35KJV

WOMEN OF GOD, SOWING SEED

Sub-Topic: How is your seed sown?

Panel Discussion

1. Seed by the Wayside
2. Seed upon the Rocks
3. Seed among Thorns
4. Seed on Good Ground

Reference Scripture: Behold, a sower went forth to sow; Matthew 13:3KJV

WOMEN OF GOD, "USING THE POWER OF GOD"

Sub-Topic: Authority — Do You Have It?

Panel Discussion

1. Difficult Situations

2. Spiritual Power

3. Overcoming Temptation

4. Miracles of Healing

Reference Scripture: But ye shall receive power after that the Holy Ghost is come upon you. Acts 1:8KJV

"GODLY WOMEN, RUNNING THE RACE IN THE 21st CENTURY"

Sub-Topic: It's a Fight to the End

Panel Discussion

1. Fighting Against Powers

2. Fighting Against Principalities

3. Fighting Against Rules of the Darkness

4. Fighting Against Spiritual Wickedness

Reference Scripture: Put on the whole armour of God that ye may be able to stand against the wiles of the devil. Ephesians 6:11KJV

WOMEN OF GOD, "VICTORIOUS IN A HOSTILE SOCIETY"

Sub-Topic: I Can Do All Things Through Christ

Panel Discussion

1. Godly Women Victorious in the Work Place
2. Godly Women, Victorious in the Home
3. Godly Women, Victorious in Society

Reference Scripture: But thanks be to God, which giveth us the victory through our Lord Jesus Christ. I Corinthians 15:57 KJV

WOMEN OF GOD, "CONQUERORS THROUGH CHRIST"

Sub-Topic: Who Shall Separate Us?

Panel Discussion

1. Tribulations

2. Distress

3. Persecution

4. Famine

Reference Scripture: Praying always with all prayer and supplications in the Spirit. Ephesians 6:18KJV

THE POWER OF PRAYER, CHANGING SITUATIONS

Sub-Topic: Take Charge!

Panel Discussion

1. Praying Against Principalities
2. Praying Against Rulers of Darkness
3. Praying Against Wickedness in High Places
4. Praying Against the Wiles of the Devil

Reference Scripture: praying always with all prayer and supplications in the Spirit. Ephesians 6:18KJV

WOMEN OF GOD, "STAND UP AND BE COUNTED"

Sub-Topic: Growing in the Word

Panel Discussion

1. Stand Up for Righteousness

2. Bind Together in Unity

3. Peace in the Midst of Strife

4. Love in Spite of

Reference Scripture: Finally my brethren, be strong in the Lord, and in the power of his might. Ephesians 6:10KJV

WOMEN OF GOD, "USING PRESCRIPTIONS FOR A GODLY LIFE"

Sub-Topic: Your Spiritual Strength

Panel Discussion

1. Let not mercy and truth forsake thee — Proverbs 3:3

2. Trust in the Lord with all thine heart — Proverbs 3:5

3. In all thy ways acknowledge him — Proverbs 3:6

4. Be not wise in thine own eyes — Proverbs 7:8

5. Honour the Lord with thy substance — Proverbs 9:10

Reference Scripture: It shall be health to thy navel, and marrow to thy bones. Proverbs 3:8 KJV

THE POWER OF PRAISE

Sub-Topic: Praise the Lord

Panel Discussion

1. Praise God In his sanctuary

2. Praise Him for his mighty acts

3. Praise Him with stringed instruments and organs

4. What is that thing called praise?

5. The benefits of praising him

Reference Scripture: And when he had consulted with the people, he appointed singers unto the Lord, and that should praise the beauty of holiness. II Chronicles 20:21KJV

WOMEN OF GOD, "EMPOWERED TO SERVE"

Sub-Topic: Equipped for Service

Panel Discussion

1. Deborah

2. Mary and Martha

3. Esther

Reference Scripture: Length of days is in her right hand, and in her left hand riches and honour. Proverbs 3:16 KJV

WOMEN IN THE WORD, CLAIMING VICTORY

Sub-Topic: Woman, Thou Art Loosed

Panel Discussion

1. Pride

2. Addictions

3. Abuse

4. Relationships

Reference Scripture: Know ye not that they which run in a race run all, but one receiveth the prize? So run that ye may obtain. I Corinthians 9:24KJV

HOLY WOMEN, BEARING FRUIT

Sub-Topic: Fruit of the Spirit

Panel Discussion

1. Love
2. Joy
3. Peace
4. Longsuffering
5. Gentleness
6. Goodness
7. Faith
8. Meekness
9. Temperance

Reference Scripture: Be not deceived; God is not mocked; for whatsoever a man soweth, that shall he also reap. Galatians 6:7KJV

WOMEN STANDING IN PRAYER

Sub-Topic: Until Something Happens

Panel Discussion

(P) pray until something happens

(U) until

(S) something

(H) happens

Reference Scripture: Pray without ceasing. I Thessalonians 5:17KJV

GODLY WOMEN, "SETTING A GOAL"

Sub-Topic: The Fight is On!

Panel Discussion

1. Purpose
2. Plan
3. Wisdom
4. Winning the Prize

Reference Scripture: I can do all things through Christ which strengtheneth me. Ephesians 4:13KJV

MISSIONARIES TOTALLY COMMITTED

Sub-Topic: Meeting God's Approval

Panel Discussion

1. Committed to Christ; humility of spirit

2. Committed to devotion and determination

3. Committed to study and spiritual strength

4. Committed to offer salvation for the human family

Reference Scripture: Let this mind be in you which was also in Christ Jesus. Philippians 2:5KJV

CRY OF A GODLY WOMAN: "LORD, TEACH US"

Sub-Topic: How to Pray

Panel Discussion

1. Preparation for Prayer

2. How to Approach the Lord

3. Guidance in Prayer

4. Blocked Channels

Reference Scripture: But when ye pray, use not vain repetitions, as the heathens do; for the think that they shall be heard from their much speaking. Matthew 6:7 KJV

THE THREE ASPECTS OF PRAYER

Sub-Topic: Communing with God

Panel Discussion

1. ASK   And it shall be Given You

2. SEEK   And ye Shall Find

3. KNOCK   And it shall be Opened Unto You

Reference Scripture: Ask, and it shall be given you; seek, and ye shall find; knock and it shall be opened unto you. Matthew 7:7KJV

PRAYER, PRAISE AND POWER TIME

Sub-Topic: It's Breakthrough Time

Panel Discussion

1. Principles of Prayer

2. Principles of Praise

3. Breaking Bread through the Word

4. The Anointing

Reference Scripture: And at midnight Paul and Silas prayed and sang praises unto God. Acts 16:25KJV

WILL THOU BE MADE WHOLE?

Sub-Topic: Hear the Word

Panel Discussion

1. Physical Healing

2. Inner Healing

3. Spiritual Healing

4. Keeping a Prayerful Mind

5. Thanksgiving and Praise

Reference Scripture: And he said unto him, arise go thy way; thy faith hath made thee whole. St. Luke 17:19KJV

WOMEN OF GOD, WEATHERING THE STORMS OF LIFE

Sub-Topic: Fully Persuaded

Panel Discussion

1. On the Mountain (Matthew 5:1)

2. Through the Fire (Jude vs. 23)

3. In the Valley (Psalms 23:4)

4. Family Distress (Luke 22:24)

Reference Scripture: Nay, in all these things we are more than conquerors through him that loved us. Romans 8:37KJV

MOURNING WOMEN IN ACTION

Sub-Topic: A Call for the Mourning Women

Panel Discussion

1. Proper Attitude   II Chronicles 7:14

2. Fasting   Daniel 9:3

3. Faith in God   James 2:17

4. Accepting the Charge   Romans 8:33

Reference Scripture: Thus saith the Lord of hosts, consider ye, and call for the mourning women, that they may come; Jeremiah 9:17aKJV

GODLY WOMEN WITH POWER, OVERCOMING TEMPTATIONS

Sub-Topic: Refusing to Compromise

Panel Discussion

1. Lust of the Eye
2. Lust of the Flesh
3. Pride of Life

Reference Scripture: For it is written, thou shalt worship the Lord they God, and him only shalt thou serve. Matthew 4:10KJV

ERNESTLY CONTEND FOR THE FAITH

Sub-Topic: Supporting the Cause

Panel Discussion

1. Steadfast in the Faith
2. Departing Not from the Faith
3. Not Willing to Compromise
4. Building up on your most Holy Faith

Reference Scripture: But ye, beloved, building up yourselves on your most holy faith, praying in the Holy Ghost. Jude vs. 20KJV

THE TOTAL WOMAN

Sub-Topic: Walking by Faith

Panel Discussion

1. Redeeming the Time

2. Building Bridges

3. Blueprint for Blessings

4. Transformed, Not Reformed.

Reference Scripture: For we walk by faith, not by sight. II Corinthians 5:7 KJV

THE CHRISTIAN WORKERS OUTFIT CLOTHED IN RIGHTEOUSNESS

Sub-Topic: Putting on the Whole Armour

Panel Discussion

1. Cheerful Giver   II Corinthians 9:7

2. Walking by Faith   II Corinthians 5:7

3. Praying Always   Ephesians 6:18

4. Studying the Word   II Timothy 2:15

Reference Scripture: And that you put on the new man. Ephesians 4:24 KJV

HOLY WOMEN OF GOD, WALKING BY FAITH!

Sub-Topic: We Walk by Faith and Not by Sight—
I Corinthians 5:7

Panel Discussion

F—ather (Abraham) established in the Faith—Hebrews 11:4

A—uthor (Jesus) living, conquering and overcoming Faith—Galatians 3:11

I—n dwelling (Holy Ghost) power of Faith.—Matthew 17:20

T—rials (perfection) patience of Faith—James 1:2-4

H—earing of the (Word of God) brings Faith—Romans 10:17

Reference Scripture: Now faith is the substance of things hope for, the evidence of things not seen. Hebrews 11:1KJV

WHAT HAVE YOU DONE FOR JESUS?

What have you done for Jesus
As you walked life's road today?
Have you spoken a word of kindness
Or taken time to pray?

For the wayward whose feet have wandered
For the weak who have suffered long,
For the heart that is weary and broken,
And somewhere has lost its song?

Have you asked for God's rich blessing
On those who preach His word,
Or told the story of Jesus' love
To those who have never heard?

What have you done for Jesus
As you trod your earthly way?
Will the world know more of the Savior's love
By the way you have lived today?

Author unknown

CONSIDER

Is anybody happier
Because you passed his way?
Does anyone remember
That you spoke to him today?

This day is almost over,
And its tolling time is through
Is there anyone to utter now,
A friendly word for you?

Can you say tonight in passing,
With the day that slipped as fast,
That you helped a single person
Of the many that you passed?

Is a single heart rejoicing,
Over what you did or said?
Does one whose hopes were fading
Now with courage look ahead?

Did you waste the day, or lose it?
Was it well or poorly spent?
Did you leave a trail of kindess
Or a scar of discontent?

Author unknown

ALMOST PERSUADED TO BE A MISSIONARY

Almost persuaded now to leave all,
Almost persuaded to answer God's call
Souls now in darkness deep long for the light and weep
Servant of God asleep, God sees it all

Almost persuaded, God's call is clear
Almost persuaded, but home is dear
Is not the cost too great?
Cannot the heathen wait?
Your answer seals the fate of precious souls

Almost persuaded, bitter remorse!
Almost persuaded, eternal loss!
Souls lost who might have been washed in the crimson stream
Dying without a gleam of gospel light

Almost persuaded. Will you obey?
Almost persuaded. Do not delay!
If you obey the call, God will be all in all
Men at his feet will fall; your joy be full

Author unknown

GET SOMEBODY ELSE

The Lord He had a job for me,
But I had so much to do,
I said: "you get somebody else,
Or wait till I get through."

One day I needed the Lord myself
Needed Him right away
And He never answered me at all,
But I could hear Him say

Down in my accusin' heart
"I've got too much to do,
Or get somebody else,
Or wait til I get through."

Now when the Lord has a job for me
I never try to skirk,
I drop what I have on my hand
And does the good Lord's work;
Nobody else can do the job
The Lord's marked out for YOU.

Author unknown

TRAVELING ON MY KNEES

Last night I took a journey
To a land far 'cross the seas;
I didn't go by boat or plane,
I traveled on my knees.
I saw so many people there
In deepest depths of sin,
And Jesus told me I should go
That there were souls to win.
But I said, "Jesus, I can't go
And work with such as these."
He answered quickly," Yes, you can
By traveling on your knees."
He said, "You pray; I'll meet the need.
You call and I will hear.
Be concerned about lost souls
Of those both far and near."
And so I tried it, knelt in prayer,
Gave up some hours of ease;
I felt the Lord right by my side
While traveling on my knees.
I can go and heed thy call
By traveling on my knees."

Author unknown